KNOWLEDGE REVIEW

Types and quality of knowledge in social care

Ray Pawson, Annette Boaz, Lesley Grayson, Andrew Long and Colin Barnes

Social Care I

Better knowledge for better practice

First published in Great Britain in November 2003 by the Social Care Institute for Excellence (SCIE)

Social Care Institute for Excellence
1st Floor
Goldings House
2 Hay's Lane
London SE1 2HB
UK
www.scie.org.uk

© Queen Mary University, London 2003

British Library Cataloguing in Publication Data

A catalogue record for this book is available from the British Library

ISBN 1 904812 02 3

Ray Pawson is Reader in the Department of Sociology and Social Policy at the University of Leeds. **Annette Boaz** is Senior Research Fellow in the UK Centre for Evidence-based Policy and Practice at Queen Mary University of London. **Lesley Grayson** works in the UK Centre for Evidence-based Policy and Practice at Queen Mary University of London. **Andrew Long** is Professor and Director of the Health Care Practice R&D Unit at the University of Salford. **Colin Barnes** is Professor of Disability Studies and Director of the Centre for Disability Studies at the University of Leeds.

Produced by The Policy Press
University of Bristol
Fourth Floor, Beacon House
Queen's Road
Bristol BS8 1QU
UK
www.policypress.org.uk

Front cover: photograph supplied by kind permission of www.JohnBirdsall.co.uk
Printed and bound in Great Britain by Hobbs the Printers Ltd, Southampton.

Contents

Preface

SCIE's commitment to reflect the wide range of groups who have a stake in social care is mirrored in its work on developing the knowledge base to underpin evidence-based social care. In particular, SCIE is determined to ensure that different kinds of evidence, from a range of different sources, is recognised, valued and built on. This brings the need to consider what types of knowledge SCIE should draw on, and how to distinguish good quality knowledge from that which should not be relied upon in policy making and practice.

We are grateful to the EvidenceNetwork team at the ESRC UK Centre for Evidence-based Policy and Practice (Queen Mary, University of London) for the current review, which takes us a significant part of the way towards achieving these goals. The review recommends a system of classifying knowledge in social care and a framework for assessing the quality of that knowledge. Most importantly, it offers a unifying vision of the contribution that different types of knowledge can make to social care, and one that SCIE can reflect in its work to develop appropriate methods of reviewing knowledge.

The review does not, of course, offer a solution for all the problems in developing the knowledge base for social care. SCIE will be taking work forward on how the classification is used in practice and on the proposed assessment framework. We look forward to collaborating with the EvidenceNetwork and others in this task.

Professor Mike Fisher
Director of Research and Reviews

Summary

This report derives from an eight-month project to explore the types and quality of social care knowledge. It is divided into two parts, and the division of labour between the two speaks for itself. **Stage One** proposes a classification of social care knowledge based on its sources: organisations, practitioners, the policy community, researchers and users and carers. It deals with 'types' – that is to say, it identifies the main forms of research, experience and wisdom that make up the social care knowledge base. **Stage Two** deals with 'quality' – that is to say, it identifies some of the standards that should be used in assessing the very different sources of knowledge that inform social care.

Stage One has seven chapters:

Chapter 1 spells out our brief to develop an intellectually defensible classification of social care knowledge that can point users towards appropriate knowledge for particular purposes, and help SCIE in its drive to construct an 'information infrastructure'. *Chapter 2* outlines our approach to the task as a preliminary to the more detailed chapters that follow. *Chapter 3* gives an overview of the massive and diverse world of social care knowledge as a prelude to our efforts to reduce it to a manageable set of categories. *Chapter 4* returns to the core requirement of the report by setting out some key features of a 'good' classification. *Chapter 5* looks at what can be learned from other classifiers and typologisers who have attempted a similar task in related domains, and describes the emergence of two classifications that looked promising for our particular purposes. *Chapter 6* explores these two classifications by applying them to a sample of abstracts from the social care literature. *Chapter 7* presents our recommendation for a classification system that captures the range of social care knowledge in a way that we believe to be simple (and therefore easy to use) and effective (in that it allows access to significant and relevant information).

Our chosen classification is based on the different *sources* of social care knowledge, identified as:

- organisational knowledge
- practitioner knowledge
- user knowledge
- research knowledge
- policy community knowledge

Several decisions informed this choice of classification system. Three key intentions, however, were that, through SCIE, the classification should send out the message that:

- all these sources have a vital role to play in building up the social care evidence base, there being no hierarchy implied in the above list;
- it is important not to neglect sources of knowledge that are tacit, that currently lack prestige and seem less compelling;
- information needs are variable, and there is flexibility and diversity within the recommended schema in order to help users find appropriate evidence for their particular requirements.

However, in proposing *sources* as the primary approach to classification, we are not ignoring the need to consider the *purposes* for which material is produced. We see *purpose* as important in understanding the type of knowledge produced, but it will normally feature at a second stage or layer of classification.

Stage Two examines how these different kinds of knowledge might be judged within a framework that respects the wide diversity of views on quality within the social care community.

Standards thinking is highly developed in only a minority of the social care knowledge sources, and the framework presented here is provisional. It requires ongoing refinement by SCIE, working with the many stakeholder groups in the social care community, if it is to evolve into a practical and generally acceptable set of tools. There are two components: six generic quality standards, and commentaries on existing or potential standards for each knowledge source.

The generic standards

These are applicable across the full spectrum of social care knowledge, underpin the more detailed source-specific standards, and have the potential to command support among all stakeholders: knowledge producers as well as users, practitioners as well as policy makers, service users as well as providers and regulators. In brief, the question to be asked of any piece of knowledge is **TAPUPAS?**

Transparency – is it open to scrutiny?
Accuracy – is it well grounded?
Purposivity – is it fit for purpose?
Utility – is it fit for use?
Propriety – is it legal and ethical?
Accessibility – is it intelligible?
Specificity – does it meet source-specific standards?

The phrasing of the generic standards as questions reflects the first key message of the report: that standards do not replace judgement. They are part of an appraisal process, providing a reference point for judgements and a context against which to explain why and how judgements are made. Once fully developed, the generic standards could be used to good effect alone as an appraisal tool, especially in areas where source-specific standards are inadequately developed.

The source-specific standards

The exceptional diversity of the social care knowledge base means that it also desirable for knowledge to meet standards operating within its particular domain. In many cases these are latent and considerable development work is needed, building on broader standards thinking within each domain.

* *Organisational knowledge:* standards, both regulatory and aspirational, abound in this knowledge source and are designed to ensure accountability and best practice in social care. These are a good starting point for developing tools to appraise organisational knowledge.
* *Practitioner knowledge:* explicit standards are rare in this source, and will only be applicable to that portion of practitioner knowledge that is documented. Standards may be adapted from those applied to

qualitative research, or derived from research on reflective practice and ways of 'articulating the unspoken'.

- *Policy community knowledge:* standards are also rare in this source, and a significant proportion of its knowledge (especially ideological and political reasoning) may not be susceptible to formal appraisal except by using some of the generic standards. However, recent work to promote 'better policy making' offers scope for developing more specific standards to judge policy community knowledge arising in the aftermath of political decisions.
- *Research knowledge:* there are many standards for the generation and critical appraisal of research knowledge, but judging the quality of knowledge in this source is not without difficulty. There are disputes about the nature and content of standards in areas such as qualitative research, and the implementation of standards is sometimes weak so that conformity with them is not necessarily a guarantee of quality.
- *User and carer knowledge:* standards for knowledge quality are rare, but show signs of emerging from concerns with accountability and participation. Given the diversity of perspectives on the role of users and carers, the chances of consensus on knowledge standards in this domain may be slim.

The diverse and incomplete picture of social care knowledge standards is summarised in a table at the end of the report. A second key message to emerge from the analysis is the interweaving of different knowledge sources in standards development. Potential standards for practitioner knowledge are emerging from the work of researchers; the principle of participation, central to the user and carer community, has permeated across to the organisational and research domains; standards from the research community on peer review and critical appraisal are attracting increasing interest within government organisations. This suggests that, in SCIE's future development of source-specific standards for knowledge appraisal, much will be gained from looking at ideas and experiences across all five sources.

Stage One:
A classification of types of knowledge in social care

1

Our brief: what SCIE wanted to know

SCIE's credo is 'better knowledge for better practice' and the purpose of our project is to take the first steps in identifying the crucial elements of knowledge that will underpin good practice in social care. The purview of 'social care' is extremely wide – consisting of the efforts of many lay and professional groups, engaging with a broad spectrum of service users and their supporters, using all manner of interventions and practices to alleviate a wide range of personal and societal problems. This state of affairs placed three requirements on our project.

1.1. Match knowledge to information need

In identifying best practice, SCIE aims to follow a 'balanced agenda'. SCIE will, of course, attend to the findings of rigorous empirical research but will also take into account the importance of first-hand experience, practical nous, and familiarity with the craft skills of social care. Accordingly, our classification system should not privilege the viewpoints of any particular stakeholder, or of any one strategy for generating knowledge. But neither should it assume that all standpoints are of equal merit on all occasions, on all issues and for all purposes. The classification's first task is to help direct users to appropriate knowledge to support each different social care function and information need.

1.2. Ensure clarity and ease of use

Another purpose of the classification is to help in the wider drive to construct an 'information infrastructure' in the form of the *electronic Library of Social Care* (*eLSC*). The information held in *eLSC* will be utilised by subject experts carrying out scholarly, systematic reviews of best practice, but it will be compiled by non-specialists and its content will also need to be comprehensible to practitioner and, perhaps, lay audiences. One of the first principles of knowledge management is that the information housed in electronic databases and retrieval systems should be simple to access and to use. The knowledge classification schema is the first point of entry into all such systems and there are some simple do's and don'ts associated with such a gateway. The key is to find a balance between 'clarity' and 'familiarity' in the terminology employed. Definitions should be precise enough to avoid ambiguity but also be expressed in straightforward terms carrying everyday meaning. Part of our remit is to strike this balance in the classification of social care knowledge.

1.3. Create a meaningful classification

Our third responsibility was to produce a classification that is 'intellectually defensible'. This is arguably the key requirement of the report but one that defies easy definition. Given that the social care knowledge base is diverse and fragmented, it would be easy to be selective and partisan in identifying and naming its crucial components. (This, incidentally, is an even more difficult test when it comes to identifying the 'standards' to which knowledge should aspire. As we will demonstrate in the second part of the report, standards are contested, sometimes quite acrimoniously.) What we have tried to do in producing a 'defensible' classification is to make the basis of our reasoning and judgement clear at all times. Our method is outlined in the next chapter and it should also be noted that this final report is a condensation of three 'starter papers', which should be consulted if the reader wishes to examine our logic in further detail:

- SCIE Starter Paper 1: *Seeing the wood for the trees* (Ray Pawson, 21 pages)
- SCIE Starter Paper 2: *SCIE-like typologies* (Ray Pawson, 16 pages)
- SCIE Starter Paper 3: *Fit for purpose* (Lesley Grayson, 9 pages)

These are also available as Numbers 12-14 in the Working Paper Series of the ESRC UK Centre for Evidence-based Policy and Practice, via http://www.evidencenetwork.org

Method: our approach to the task

We employed the following design and division of labour.

2.1. Preliminary (scoping) search of the literature

We began by amassing a selection of literature that would provide an indication of the breadth and depth of the varied approaches to social care. We were particularly interested in sources that laid claim to provide an 'approach', a 'perspective', a 'paradigm', a 'standpoint', an 'outlook' on social care. In other words, we tried to build a self-portrait – how did social care define itself, how did it distinguish its own tribes, and how did it explain its boundaries?

2.2. Initial exploration of the field

A thorough reading and analysis of this literature then allowed us to begin to construct some potential 'types' of social care knowledge. Our approach at this stage was to construct a wide-ranging 'checklist' of social care perspectives rather than a classification system. This identified over a dozen types and scores of prospective subtypes, and prompted some initial thinking on degrees of 'family resemblance' that might contribute to a tighter classification. The process is sketched in Chapter 3 and set down in further detail, with full bibliographic references, in Starter Paper 1.

2.3. Search for existing classifications and typologies

The next task was to reduce this crude inventory to a classification of manageable proportions. In order to do this we consulted the literature on 'classifications and measurement systems' for some key pointers and examined some existing typologies and classifications within fields related to social care. This search failed to reveal any previous attempt that corresponded exactly with our own task although there were available classifications of various portions of the overall field. These are analysed in Chapter 5 and set down in detail, with bibliographic references, in Starter Paper 2.

2.4. Comparison of the strengths and weaknesses of different classification systems

Classification systems are always simplifications and approximations, and none of those we identified was comprehensive enough to encapsulate the whole spectrum of social care knowledge. With these weaknesses in mind, we proceeded to adapt and extend the more useful systems in order to arrive at a classification of our own. Our benchmark was that all the major forms of social care knowledge should be accommodated, without there being any substantial overlap between the categories. This process is described in detail in Starter Paper 2.

2.5. Applying the classifications

This process enabled us to arrive at what we considered to be two intellectually defensible classification systems. One was based on 'sources' of social care knowledge and the other on 'purposes', that is to say the aims and intention of the particular body of knowledge (for example, organisational improvement or changing oppressive structures). A choice had to be made between the two potential systems in the context of our remit to produce a classification capable of supporting a user-friendly information system. To explore this feature, we conducted a small pilot exercise to try and categorise a set of social care reports using the rival systems, a process that produced a clear winner in the 'sources' approach. The process is outlined in Chapter 6, and described more fully in Starter Paper 3.

2.6. Consultation process to hone the final classification

A final feature of our method was the consultative processes that underpinned all stages of the project. SCIE hopes to forge a 'constructive consensus' on what counts as social care knowledge, and building accord was also part of our method for honing the classification. This was/is being achieved at various levels. Our team was assembled to represent some of the vying interests in social care, and developing typologies is an iterative process. We would like to acknowledge the contributions of colleagues from policy, practice and academia who have commented on early drafts of the Starter Papers.

In particular we would like to thank the 19 representatives from the service user community who attended a day-long workshop at SCIE and provided very useful feedback on the emerging typology. A full report[1] has been delivered to the organisations involved which spanned agencies both of and for children, parents of disabled children, informal carers, disabled people, people with learning difficulties, mental health service users and survivors, and minority ethnic groups.

The day's events included short presentations from Mike Fisher of SCIE and Ray Pawson of the research team, two workshops on aspects of the research process, two feedback sessions, and a concluding plenary session on the strengths and weaknesses of the project. Key messages to emerge were:

- the future generation of social care knowledge must be far more responsive to, and reflective of, the diversity of service users' views;
- all research strategies, regardless of origin, should be judged by the same standards or criteria;
- the standards used to judge the quality of user-controlled research should be used to judge the quality of all research strategies used to generate knowledge in the social care field.

3

Dealing with complexity: the diverse world of social care

This chapter reproduces the initial overview of types of knowledge in social care produced by simply 'trawling' though the available literature. The presentation throws up an awkward paradox in that its purpose is to capture enormity of scope, and this has to be accomplished via a brief summary. Accordingly, what follows is a pocket checklist of 'candidate' knowledge forms. Each is, in some important sense, a distinctive 'tradition' within social care. Each maintains its own expertise, methods, purposes, standards etc. Each is prone to carry internal subdivisions and there is both overlap and contention between the various factions. Interested readers might like to consult Starter Paper 1 for further details and references, noting that even that document does not claim to be entirely comprehensive.

- *Experimental and quasi-experimental approaches*: the first of these tests out the effectiveness of social care programmes using randomised controlled trials (RCTs). This method is regarded, by its advocates, as the most objective knowledge base in social care but its use is mainly confined to therapeutic/psychiatric interventions. There are a number of less powerful quasi-experimental designs that can be used on the (frequent) occasions when it is impossible to allocate clients to treatments by random allocation.
- *Measuring and monitoring*: there is a huge amount of research and practical activity aimed at assessing, diagnosing, gauging, scoring and weighing up key issues in the social care field. These are spread right across from measures of the nature of the problem ('inputs') to the monitoring of the effects of provision ('outputs'). They include 'risk assessment', 'deprivation indices', 'quality of life assessments' etc.
- *Consultation*: this is an approach aimed at building consensual knowledge between service providers and other stakeholders. Its function is to provide ground rules for new agencies, regulations, codes of practice, service frameworks etc. Methods of consultation include

'formal surveys', 'citizen's juries', 'deliberative discussions', 'focus groups', 'talk shops', 'health impact assessments' and so on.

- *Qualitative and case study research:* this refers to the mountain of reports on the first-hand experience of practitioners or users of social care. These include: academic pieces in the 'phenomenological' tradition; in-house reports on project implementation; journalistic pieces providing self-reflection; campaigning testimony allowing individuals to tell their stories. What unites them is the commitment to articulating the tacit wisdom of everyday social care.

- *Action research:* this is another form of research-based knowledge. It has a particularly venerable place in social care, given its fragmented and localised practices. It is based on a melding of roles, being conducted by 'researcher-practitioners'. It also features the 'action research cycle', whereby findings are directly and systematically incorporated into organisational reform and practice modification.

- *Emancipatory and user-led approaches:* these prioritise the standpoint of the social care user, arguing, in the strongest version, that users are oppressed and that an oppressive reality cannot be understood by 'experts' but only by the objects of oppression. It takes two forms: 'user led-research' in which all features of the conduct of inquiry are controlled by users, and 'anti-oppressive practice' which campaigns to carry user perspectives into all other forms of social care knowledge.

- *Process evaluation:* this is a qualitative approach to programme evaluation. It is assumed that social care interventions are complex and pass through many hands, creating knowledge about implementation chains. Process evaluation thus investigates the key stepping stones of an intervention and how the vital ingredients can be activated to ensure programme success.

- *Audit and inspection:* these provide knowledge to better regulate and bring accountability to the services that deliver social care. They operate at the 'macro' level, with whole institutions, geographical areas or modes of provision being appraised for management purposes. Their methodology trades on 'performance measurement', 'benchmarking', 'assessment frameworks' and so on. Inspection carries the crucial additional aspect of the 'site visit' to examine individual and team performance, and organisational processes.

- *Legal provisions and public inquiries:* social care is tightly regulated and legal provisions constitute a major restraining influence on practice. Following some high profile public inquiries, these too have come to impose strict obligations on social care practice. They provide what might be thought of as 'infrastructural' knowledge, namely the legislative frameworks, case law, organisational principles and regulations that influence the basic operation and role of social care.

- *Systematic review and meta-analysis*: reviews of existing evidence have become the instrument of choice in evidence-based policy and practice. Similar initiatives are tried and tried again, and researched and researched again, prompting the development of methods of secondary analysis whose task is to stack up that evidence. In social care it is an embryonic form of knowledge, there being no established way of marshalling together evidence from the diverse sources outlined here.

- *Post-modern and dialogic approaches*: from this perspective, it is impossible to separate the validity of claims to knowledge from the standpoint of those making the declarations. Certain forms of understanding tend to prevail in social care because of the power of their producers. Promoting 'marginalised' discourses in social care is thus part of the post-modernising project. On this view, however, there is no neutral vantage point from which to value knowledge. The very idea of the rational extraction of 'best practices' from the evidence is anathema to this perspective.

- *Tacit knowledge, practice wisdom, experiential learning*: tacit wisdom has long been celebrated as a vital part of the knowledge repertoire in social care. Ostensibly intuitive practices are actually based on the theories taught within education and training, knowledge gained from watching what colleagues do, trial and error, reflective practice, peer approval, client satisfaction and so on. Such personal and private contemplation is hard to capture in an evidence base but it does find a place in training and experiential learning. It is also formalised as the 'oral tradition' becomes set down in research and other publications.

- *A.N. Others*: this is the residual category capturing additional forms of knowledge. It is the bête noire of classifiers – but inevitable. For instance, there are forms of evaluation research such as the 'single case' approach or the 'theory-driven' strategy that do not really slot in to the above, although there are at least three categories that describe evaluation research. Other knowledge frameworks that inform social care are not present at all in the preliminary list such as those based on 'ethical' or 'spiritual' considerations. Another conundrum is set by 'mixed-method' research which deliberately straddles the schedule of strategies. Another voluminous omission is the 'policy thought piece', which trades on conceptual and ideological dimensions of knowledge.

We reproduce this miniature sketch of the landscape to illustrate the dilemmas of reaching a final classification of social care knowledge. As our residual category illustrates, it would be certainly possible to extend the schema to a score or more categories. Many of the groupings above contain subtypes (for example, audit and inspection) which are arguably distinctive and better managed with a further elaboration of the schema.

But we have to be straightforward. A twenty-fold classification would be of no use to anyone, so we have to purge rather than embellish. One route is to eliminate categories altogether. One could argue that 'post-modernism' or 'spiritual' approaches are antithetical to evidence-based policy and practice, and can be ignored. One could argue that 'tacit knowledge' and the 'policy thought pieces', almost by definition, can never be captured as 'evidence'. Against this is SCIE's injunction to be comprehensive in order to reflect the broad base of social care knowledge. It is clear that achieving a more user-friendly set of categories requires that we simplify and condense and to this task we now turn, first by outlining some general principles of classification.

Classifications and typologies: hows, whys and wherefores

A classification system takes a body of information and divides it into the most prominent subtypes. Let us call these:

A   B   C   D   E   F

There are several 'rules' about how this is best achieved, the principal ones being that:

- *The categories should be totally inclusive:* they should cover all the significant sub-sets of the activity in question. That is to say, it should be impossible to find an instance that is not either an **A** or a **B** or a **C** or a **D** or an **E** or a **F**.
- *The categories should be mutually exclusive:* there should be no significant overlap between the sub-sets identified. It should not be possible for a particular case to be both **A** and **B**, or both **A** and **C**, or both **D** and **F**, still less both **B** and **E** and **F**.

Many bodies of information are so complex that there is scant possibility of describing their diversity in terms of a handful of categories as in the simple illustration above. Complexity may be added in two ways. The first is to acknowledge that each category contains sub-types. Thus **'A'** is made up of several sub-types a_1, a_2, a_3 and so on. The classification thus takes on a 'roots' structure, illustrated schematically in Figure 1.

Yet further complexity can be added by acknowledging that each of the sub-types yields still further differences. The 'roots' thus deepen still further, illustrated above with some sub-sub-sets of **'C'**.

Another way of producing a more comprehensive classification is to transform it into a 'typology'. This begins with the primary classification as before but also describes a further set of properties of each sub-type. These are produced in the form of a matrix in which the main categories (**A**, **B**, **C**, **D**, **E** and **F**) are arrayed on the horizontal axis as before. The

Figure 1: A 'roots' classification

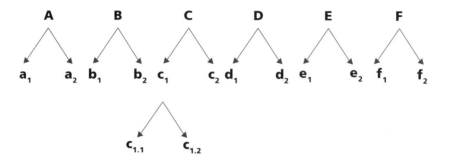

secondary characteristics or properties (1, 2, 3, 4, 5 etc) of each type are then displayed on the vertical axis as in Figure 2.

This device produces a potential information framework of considerable elegance. Reading across the cell entries allows one to compare how each major category functions in terms of each secondary characteristic. In the example, we see that **A** and **B** are identical on property 1, that **C**, **D** and **E** together take on a different form, and that **F** has a unique configuration.

Figure 2: An information matrix in the form of a typology

	A	B	C	D	E	F
1	x	x	y	y	y	z
2						
3						
4						
5						

We debated the merits of each type of framework for our classification of social care knowledge. In the end, we recommend a simple 'roots' style, recognising five main types and a limited array of sub-types. The reasoning behind the choice will become clear as the report progresses, but in formal terms the decisive factors are:

- *Complexity:* social care is a broad church, both in terms of its types of knowledge and their characteristics. Put schematically, this means that rather than stretching from 'A to F' the knowledge types actually span 'A to Z'; and that rather than covering '1 to 5' their properties actually run from '1 to 100'. The trim typology of Figure 2 is thus rather illusory and attempting to imitate it risks over-compression in representing the diverse activities that constitute social care.
- *Discontinuity:* the idea of reading across the rows of the typology in order to compare the properties of different forms of knowledge is also rather misleading. Social care operates with such different perspectives, put to such different ends, that such an exercise would have produced many blanks. For instance, many of the technical properties needed to describe 'research'-based knowledge would be quite irrelevant in classifying forms of knowledge that were 'administrative' in function.
- *Utility:* our major reason for preferring the simpler form of classification relates to the demands of information systems. The more elaborate the system the more difficult it is to marshal and use, and it is unlikely that *eLSC* (or its users) could easily employ a matrix style information framework.

In short, we advise against trying to achieve a classification that compresses both types of knowledge and their properties in one fell swoop. We have taken a one-step-at-a-time approach, attempting:

1. to arrive at the cleanest possible classification of the essential forms of social care knowledge;
2. to make a modest initial mapping of some of the key sub-types of these main forms;
3. to forego the task of listing and compressing the properties and characteristics of each type, and to investigate their differences via the issue of standards.

Now we move from the general to the particular, exploring some earlier attempts to classify the complex world of social care knowledge.

5

Comparing notes: previous attempts at knowledge classification

The simplest forms of classification are attained by dint of being 'unidimensional'. This means that just one feature is attended to in building the classification. Now, in our ad hoc classification in Chapter 3, several characteristics are blended in the identification of the types. Sometimes they are distinguished by 'research technique' (for example, RCTs); sometimes they are marked by 'philosophical orientation' (for example, post-modernism); sometimes they are characterised by their originator (for example, practitioner-researchers); sometimes they are identified by 'purpose' (for example, performance management); sometimes they are defined by their 'medium' (for example, the oral tradition); sometimes they are labelled by their 'source' (for example, legal tribunals).

Invariably, the pen pictures above have called on an admixture of these features in order to give a rounded portrait of each type. To facilitate the construction of a simpler classification, we need to select from these options to arrive at one dimension that will traverse all the forms of social care knowledge and yet leave us with a manageable set of categories.

In order to achieve this we examined some existing classifications and typologies for exemplars and pointers. Which underlying dimension would achieve a comprehensive yet manageable set of categories? This exercise is described in detail in Starter Paper 2, and the summary here excludes references to authors and sources. Our search revealed no existing schema that covered the entire range of social care knowledge. Rather, there were many classifications encapsulating parts of its territory and we sought to examine which of these had the capacity for extension over the whole of social care. Four of them are contemplated here.

5.1. Methods-based

There were several classifications and typologies based on 'research method'. Some of these referred to 'social work research', some to 'evaluative research', some to 'action research' and so on. Some identified the key divisions in terms of 'research technique' and some in terms of 'research philosophy'. Such research classifications offered us the capacity to order and reorder some of the categories put forward in the previous chapters (for example, RCTs and performance monitoring could be labelled positivism; action research and user-led research could be brought under the same umbrella). However, it rather stretched credulity to imagine that a 'research method' classification could be extended to cover, say, 'tacit knowledge' or 'legal frameworks'. Indeed, so much social care knowledge falls outside what can be thought of as 'types of research' that we cannot recommend it as the backbone of the classification.

5.2. Practice-based

Another set of classifications was based on identifying the key forms of 'social care practice'. Again, these were diverse. Some of them referred to the different types of client groups, some to types of interventions, and some to the types of problem tackled by the interventions. This range of interpretations raised the first note of caution in contemplating 'practices' as the underlying dimension of a social care classification. It is just too multifarious a concept to offer a simple organising framework. And, as with 'methods', there are forms of social care knowledge that extend beyond its remit. Much of the literature does not sit comfortably with the idea that it is aimed at a particular mode of practice. For instance, much legislative provision and much administrative data seek to establish an organisational framework for social care rather than evidence to guide its specific practices.

5.3. Purpose-based

Another popular framework found in existing classifications used 'purpose' as the underlying dimension. These were predominantly typologies of evaluative research, attempting to pigeonhole the different purposes to which it is put. For instance, one can undertake research to identify problems, develop solutions, devise and fine-tune interventions, oversee their implementation, and assess their impact. This approach seems a more promising basis for the SCIE classification, with the potential to cover and reflect the very different goals of social care. It could be extended well beyond research-based knowledge – since tacit knowledge has a purpose, tribunals have a purpose, user emancipation is a purpose, and so on. Finally, it promises a useful framework in thinking ahead to the issue of *standards* in that these could be identified in terms of what factors make a source 'fit for purpose'.

5.4. Source-based

Yet another way of classifying knowledge is to identify its 'source', and this approach can also be found in typologies of social care. As with any other service, social care has its big battalions – its policy makers, its practitioners, its users, its managers, its researchers etc. Such constituencies are not simply defined by institutional location but are also identified in terms of their knowledge. Each source generates a different type of understanding of social care and tends to be the initial consumer of the said information. Using such a framework again offers advantages for SCIE. One driving idea behind this approach is to take heed of, and make heard, the very different voices that possess social care knowledge. And for classification purposes, we can be assured that all knowledge has a source so that we can be sure that the framework will be inclusive. What is more, 'source' promises to be easy to use because much of the literature is easily traced by institutional affiliation.

With these reasons in mind we propose the 'purposes' and 'sources' based schemas as the serious contenders for the SCIE classification. Arriving at the optimal subdivisions for each classification was our final task – preceded, of course, by a decision on which mode to prefer.

6

Trying it out: applying the classifications

Our two candidate classifications are presented in summary form on page 22.

Our chosen method of deciding between Routes 1 and 2 was the attempted consensus classification of 50 recent social care papers selected from two bibliographic databases (ASSIA and Planex), using the detail provided by generally short and indicative abstracts. Starter Paper 3[2] illustrates the process, and one example is reproduced here:

> Wenger, G.C. and Tucker, I. (2002) 'Using network variation in practice: identification of support network type', *Heath and Social Care in the Community*, vol 10, no 1, January, pp 28-35.
>
> Evaluates the use of a support network measurement instrument (PANT) in social work practice, focusing primarily on a study of the introduction and use of the instrument with social work teams. The findings show how growth in familiarity with the new tool and support from managers overcame early resistance and contributed to both practitioners' confidence and understanding of the situations of older people. It allowed them to tailor interventions appropriately. (Original abstract – amended.)

The **purpose** of the work reported in this article seems to be *programme and organisational improvement*. It is concerned with an 'action approach' – the use of a tool, combined with management support, to help social workers improve their understanding of, and practice with, elderly people. However, the term 'evaluates' is also used, indicating that it might fit more appropriately into *evaluation of programme effectiveness* (with the caveat that this is an evaluation of an 'instrument' rather than a programme) if the article is the product of formal research. The use of the term 'study' suggests that this might be the case, but there is no conclusive proof in the abstract. The article could equally well fit into *circulating tacit wisdom for practical decisions* if it is a more informal description or commentary

Route 1: A classification based on the purposes of knowledge

Purpose 1 Proactive assessment and trouble shooting	Purpose 2 Programme and organisational improvement	Purpose 3 Emancipatory research and promoting user control	Purpose 4 Oversight, monitoring and compliance	Purpose 5 Evaluation of programme effectiveness	Purpose 6 Circulating tacit wisdom for practical decisions	Purpose 7 Testing social science theory for knowledge development
Measures to assess client needs, identify problem sources and chart existing best practice	*Action approaches to clarify, improve and develop ongoing practice*	*Empowerment of users by adopting their values and changing oppressive structures*	*Information management for benchmarking auditing and regulating provision*	*Formal research to discover what works, why, when and wherefore*	*Promoting skills, reflexive judgement and active decision making though experience and training*	*Generating concepts and general propositions to enlighten the policy community*

Route 2: A classification based on the sources of knowledge

Source 1 Organisational knowledge gained from management and governance of social care	Source 2 Practitioner knowledge gained from the conduct of social care	Source 3 Policy community knowledge gained from wider policy environment	Source 4 Research knowledge gathered systematically with predetermined design	Source 5 User knowledge gained from experience of service use and reflection thereupon

by those directly involved who want to share their experience of a promising practice innovation. Finally, it could fit into *oversight, monitoring and compliance* if the content is more in the nature of an organisational audit of the use of the new tool.

The **source** of the work reported in this particular article is almost certainly the empirical research community, although this is not apparent from the abstract. It could be easily ascertained by skimming the full text.

A similar pattern of complexity (Route 1) and simplicity (Route 2) was evident with our other classification attempts, and we concluded that: *Route 1* was difficult to use. Lack of detail in the abstracts was an obvious hindrance to decision making, and classification will often require a complete reading or detailed skimming of the full article. This is an important practical point if the classification is to be used as a tool by *eLSC/Caredata* staff. Abstractors and indexers rely heavily on author abstracts and rapid skimming of text in their work. If detailed reading is needed for classification purposes, there could be significant resource implications.

Multiple classifications are likely to be needed for many documents, especially books, reports and other more substantial sources of information covering a range of purposes. This may reflect some of the realities of the social care literature, but does not send simple messages to policy makers, practitioners and other users of the literature

Route 2 was much simpler to use, although we applied it only at its current basic level of development. The primary categories were clearly defined, easy to understand, and provided unambiguous single classifications after a rapid skimming of each paper. For example, the Wenger paper discussed above fits clearly into Source 4: research knowledge gathered systematically with pre-determined design.

Identifying the appropriate source category may not always be so straightforward and, in some cases, papers may need to be read in some depth. Applying Route 2 at lower levels (for example, by identifying the knowledge 'processes' employed by a particular source) will also require more detailed judgements based on a closer reading of the text. However, both involve relatively straightforward judgements of fact rather than the judgements of intent required by the purpose-based approach.

The application of the two routes to a small sample of abstracts leads us to the conclusion that the sources-based approach is sufficiently powerful to provide the basis for a classification of types of knowledge in social care. It is important to remember that this approach involves reference to the domains in which information is generated and used.

Classification is not simply an intellectual exercise; its ultimate purpose is to produce a tool for organising, understanding and accessing knowledge. In this respect, the clarity and simplicity of the sources-based approach are major advantages. In addition, it originates from research by a practising social worker. As such, it is reasonable to assume that the advantages of clarity and simplicity are further enhanced by a closer fit with the ways of thinking of practitioners (SCIE's major constituency) than classifications originating from the academic community.

By placing all potential sources of knowledge side by side at the entry point to the social care literature, this approach sends a powerful message that *all* are of potential value. It does not privilege one type of evidence above another, but nor does it preclude the possibility of making quality judgements about particular pieces of evidence within each source.

7

Conclusion: a recommended classification for knowledge in social care

The source-based approach to classification has the dual advantage of simplicity and clarity at the entry point, combined with the potential for considerable detail at lower levels. However, the source-based approach should not be regarded as a single, simple solution to the complex problem of classifying knowledge: in view of the importance of purpose in understanding the type of knowledge produced, it will normally be appropriate, at a second stage or layer of classification, to link source with purpose in some form.

For example, each source category could be further subdivided on the basis of 'purpose' although, as indicated in this report, this is not likely to be an easy process. Alternatively, the first stage of subdivision could be based on the 'process' through which knowledge is created (for example, audit, review, survey, trial, evaluation), or the 'vehicle' through which it is disseminated (for example, text book, training package, peer reviewed journal paper, guideline, campaigning document). The final choice between these and other options for developing the classification will be dependent on SCIE achieving a measure of consensus among social care knowledge-users whose needs and preferences are likely to vary.

Here we conclude by spelling out in a little more detail the primary categories of the source-based classification.

Source 1. Organisational knowledge: all modern organisations engage in governance and regulation, and these activities provide the broad knowledge frameworks that shape social care. Such materials furnish an overview of the operation of social services in the wider contexts of government agencies, local and regional authorities, and local communities.

Source 2. Practitioner knowledge: social care is conducted through the medium of practitioners' knowledge. Some of this is quite tacit and based on the social worker's or probation officer's experience of dealing, over and again, with clients from similar backgrounds, facing similar problems. Practitioner knowledge tends to be personal and context-specific and, therefore, difficult to surface, articulate and aggregate.

Source 3. User knowledge: users of social care services are not passive recipients of 'treatment' but active participants in their own 'care'. They posses vital knowledge gained from first-hand usage of, and reflection on, interventions. This knowledge, once again, also tends to remain unspoken and undervalued.

Type 4. Research knowledge: among the most palpable sources of social care knowledge is that derived from empirical inquiries based on predetermined research strategies. These provide the reports, evaluations, assessments, measures and so forth, which are the most orthodox item in any evidence base. The social care database needs to respond, however, to the particularly broad church of perspectives and paradigms that make up its research base.

Type 5. Policy community knowledge: this category sets social care in its wider policy context. Despite its diversity, social care can be thought of as one set of provisions among dozens of others made available by the public and voluntary sectors. Vital knowledge about the organisation and implementation of services thus exists in the broader policy community of ministries, civil service, think tanks and agencies.

Stage Two of the report moves on from classification to consider how knowledge from these five different sources might be assessed within a framework that respects the wide diversity of views on quality within the social care community.

Stage Two:
Towards the quality assessment of knowledge in social care

8

Introduction

This part of the report extends the investigation to develop ways of assessing the quality of the different types of knowledge within the classification outlined in Stage One.

To recap briefly, Stage One[3] involved an exploration of the social care literature to identify types of knowledge, and examine what existing classification approaches had to offer for the purposes of the SCIE project. This resulted in two possibilities: a classification based on the *purposes* of knowledge and a classification based on the *sources* of knowledge. Application to a sample of social care papers indicated that the *sources* approach was the more practical, and had the additional benefits of clarity and simplicity. This classification also has the advantage of signalling to the social care research, policy and practice communities: that *all* sources of knowledge are of potential value.

The brief for Stage Two was to provide guidance on an appropriate and feasible quality assessment framework to encompass these widely varying sources of knowledge and to develop methods of assessing quality relevant to each one. The approach used is described in the next chapter, and the remainder of the report deals, in turn, with:

- some basic issues to be considered in developing an appropriate standards regime for social care knowledge (Chapter 10);
- an overall quality standards framework that encompasses six generic, or core, standards which underpin specific standards for each source (Chapter 11);
- an exploration of ideas for standards in each of the five sources (Chapters 12-16);
- conclusions (Chapter 17).

Although much ground is covered, the framework and advice on standards are by no means comprehensive. We make no apology for pointing out that the exercise we were set is infinite. The number of activities that comprise social care, and the number of existing and potential standards that could be used or adapted for the quality appraisal of knowledge, are legion. Ours is a skeleton which we hope that SCIE can flesh out, with the wider social care community, in its future programme of work.

Figure 3: A recapitulation of knowledge sources from Stage One

Source 1	Source 2	Source 3	Source 4	Source 5
Organisational knowledge gained from management and governance of social care	Practitioner knowledge gained from the conduct of social care	Policy community knowledge gained from wider policy environment	Research knowledge gathered systematically with predetermined design	User and carer knowledge gained from experience of service use and reflection thereupon

9

Approach to the task

9.1. A preliminary search for documents referring to standards in the five knowledge sources

This built on material already discovered in Stage One, and focused on work that reflected on and/or applied a methodological appraisal of the process of developing and using standards. In addition we searched the Internet (Google), ASSIA, Social Sciences Citation Index and Caredata using terms such as 'quality', 'standards', 'appraisal', 'guidelines', 'best practice', and 'toolkits'.

Given the brief relating to the whole of social care knowledge the potential scale of this exercise was huge, even with this very limited number of sources. We were not simply searching for quality/appraisal/standards in the familiar domain of research but also in areas like practitioner knowledge which are effectively standards-free, and in others such as organisational knowledge where standards do exist but are not specifically related to knowledge. In many cases we were looking for allusions or hints or ideas rather than substantive material on 'standards in knowledge source X'.

Any attempt to apply the exhaustive search techniques typical of systematic review would have delivered unmanageable amounts of often irrelevant information. We therefore employed a 'snowball' approach of following up promising leads rather than trying to capture all potentially relevant material. This element of our work was no more than 'dipping a toe in the water', but this was inevitable given the limited time span of the project and the technical challenges of identifying relevant literature through conventional search techniques. For example:

• Social science databases do not generally index or abstract methodological concepts and where they do, it is often done inconsistently. Both abstracting and indexing are often inadequate for comprehensive information retrieval.

- Free text searches on terms such as quality, standard★, apprais★, assess★, evaluat★, review★ deliver an enormous number of irrelevant hits because all these terms are in general, non-technical usage by authors and abstractors.
- At the same time such searches miss potentially relevant material in which concepts of quality or standards are discussed but not directly referred to.

9.2. The initial mapping of standards against the knowledge sources

This also proved far from straightforward. Some of the material was generic in nature, with authors musing upon general expectations of quality frameworks; and some crossed the divide between sources, providing standards that referred, for instance, to both 'user' and 'research' knowledge. The main difficulty, however, was the stubborn lopsidedness of the material. Standards thinking is highly developed within the 'research' and 'organisational' communities but it is much harder to find materials relevant to other types of knowledge. This no doubt reflects the infancy and difficulty of work on quality appraisal in these areas.

9.3. The interrogation of (a sub-set) of potential standards material from each knowledge source

This initially took the form of familiarisation with the nature of standards across the different sources, a phase of some importance in itself. The report sets out, in simple descriptive terms, the 'state of play' on the development of standards across the different knowledge sources in social care.

9.4. The application of a more critical perspective to the emerging standards[4]

This varies considerably across the knowledge sources. For the plethora of well-defined research standards it is a case of concentrating on their use and application. For sources in which standards are embryonic, the aim is to establish some first principles, before exploring their potential development and implications for future use.

9.5. The development of an overarching framework for the standards

The aim is to provide SCIE with a tool for use as part of a knowledge management strategy for social care. Although as yet only sketched, its originality lies in beginning and enabling the comparison of standards development and usage within and across the five knowledge sources.

10

What kind of quality system is appropriate?

Prior to the development of specific standards for each knowledge source it is important to address a crucial issue highlighted in the research brief, namely: 'what kind of assessment system is appropriate?'. There is a huge diversity of views about quality within social care, and this chapter identifies some of the issues SCIE will need to consider in fostering realistic expectations about what a standards regime can and cannot cover.

• SCIE should expect some contradiction and conflict within the standards framework. There is a limit to which dispute about what constitutes good practice can or should be hidden, but it may be handled to some extent by adopting a 'fit for purpose' ethos in which particular knowledge claims are judged by the apposite standards.

• Research standards are often expressed as formulae and checklists to be applied to written documents. This may be the most appropriate model for SCIE's research activities, but it places limits on the applicability and usage of a broad quality framework. Standards also operate in and through training, experience, policy development, tacit wisdom, professional practice and so on, and many of these activities are the responsibility of other social care agencies. They are beyond the remit of this report, but there is a case for further attention to be paid to the boundary between standards-on-paper and standards-in-practice.

• Standards are developed and used for very different purposes, ranging from aspirational standards at one end of the spectrum to regulatory standards at the other. Thus 'standards' as a term is often unhelpful and, in some instances, resented. It might be more constructive to think in terms of related sets of quality concepts ranging from 'principles' to 'exemplars' to 'markers' to 'indicators' and so on. This report continues to refer to standards, although by the end the ambition is to instil the notion of an appraisal process.

- Standards are sometimes considered the enemy of intuition and inspiration. Very few of those that have been uncovered attempt or have the capacity to provide instant verdicts on the quality of knowledge. The framework is thus a permissive one, requiring skill and judgement in its application.
- This exercise has identified several examples of how the aspirations of those attempting to lay down standards for a particular activity outstrip the working assumptions of those engaged in its practice. This suggests that SCIE will need to balance the exposition of standards with a great deal of careful explanation of their limited sway, authority and longevity.
- Although SCIE can expect to deliver a broadly based standards framework, it should be appreciated that there are some important types of knowledge – notably in the ideological and political realms – that lie beyond its compass. The choice between creeds is not something that can be appraised against a quality criterion. Standards can be applied to the aftermath of political decisions. Thus the framework is intended to apply, broadly speaking, to the development, implementation and practice of social care policy.

11

Towards a quality standards framework

There are certain principles that apply to any standard setting exercise. Before looking at the specific knowledge sources, six 'generic standards', extracted and reduced from the literature, are introduced. They have the potential to command wide support across the highly varied social care community – knowledge producers as well as users, practitioners as well as policy makers, service users as well as providers and regulators – and might be thought of as the elemental standards underlying all standards. They insist on evidence rather than assertion, and require that knowledge claims should not exceed the evidence[5].

SCIE is urged to consider them for three reasons. Firstly, a not insignificant proportion of writing about social care struggles in the face of even these basic requirements, and its quality assessment cannot realistically be conducted other than at the generic level. Secondly, standards concerning methodological quality often appear to have priority and, occasionally, exclusivity in the appraisal process. In practice, these have a limited compass, and the generic standards help in the development of a tool with more universal application. Thirdly, they underpin the source-specific standards and should form a solid foundation for the ongoing discussions on knowledge quality that this report hopes to stimulate.

11.1. Generic standards

In each of the generic standards, the basic working principle is expressed as a 'should' statement, with very short examples to orient the reader to the underlying theme. These are selected from across the knowledge sources and provide some basic questions that might be asked of particular source materials. The generic standards framework requires further elaboration, application and refinement before it can be used directly for knowledge appraisal. But it is a useful first step in orienting the social care community to the kinds of questions to be raised in the appraisal process.

11.1.1. Transparency

Principle: the process of knowledge generation should be open to outside scrutiny. For knowledge to meet this standard, it should make plain how it was generated, clarifying aims, objectives and all the steps of the subsequent argument, so giving readers access to a common understanding of the underlying reasoning.
   Examples:
- A record of the case notes of a mental health practitioner – does it give the reasoning behind a recommended course of action?
- A qualitative research report on adoption – does it give full details of how the study was conducted, who was involved and what techniques were used in the analysis?

11.1.2. Accuracy

Principle: all knowledge claims should be supported by and faithful to the events, experiences, informants and sources used in their production. For knowledge to meet this standard, it should demonstrate that all assertions, conclusions, and recommendations are based on relevant and appropriate information.
   Examples:
- A group produces a report that purports to convey users' experiences of home care services – are the users' perspectives merely asserted, or is their voice clearly reported in the data and reflected in the analysis?
- A policy document is produced that claims to be a comprehensive review of existing legislation on adoption – is the coverage and analysis of previous legislation selective or all-inclusive?

11.1.3. Purposivity

Principle: the approaches and methods used to gain knowledge should be appropriate to the task in hand, or 'fit for purpose'. For knowledge to meet this standard, it should demonstrate that the inquiry has followed the apposite approach to meet the stated objectives of the exercise.

Examples:

- A local authority publishes a strategy that claims to measure changes in take-up resulting from a new residential care services regime – is an audit using standardised participation indicators applied before and after the change more appropriate than a satisfaction survey or practitioner case notes?
- A policy development team commissions a report to improve the implementation details of community sentencing – would a process evaluation fit the bill more readily than an academic 'think piece' or an inspection report?

11.1.4. Utility

Principle: knowledge should be appropriate to the decision setting in which it is intended to be used, and to the information need expressed by the seeker after knowledge. For knowledge to meet this standard it should be 'fit for use', providing answers that are as closely matched as possible to the question.

Examples:

- Practitioners are looking for knowledge on how to help first-generation immigrant families suffering from alcohol-related problems – do they need to consider just the disorder or should they also call on information sensitive to the background, history, culture and context of the clients?
- A senior child care manager is considering the balance between residential and community-based services over the next decade – would a Green/White Paper or the report of an influential think tank be more useful than the results of Best Value reviews or the results of user surveys?

11.1.5. Propriety

Principle: knowledge should be created and managed legally, ethically and with due care to all relevant stakeholders. For knowledge to meet this standard, it should present adequate evidence, appropriate to each point of contact, of the informed consent of relevant stakeholders. The release (or withholding) of information should also be subject to agreement.

Examples:

- A carer's group shares information about members with other organisations – has there been consent from all the members concerned?
- A government department consults regularly with the same community – has it considered or used results from previous exercises, and can this be demonstrated?

11.1.6. Accessibility

Principle: knowledge should be presented in a way that meets the needs of the knowledge seeker. To meet this standard, no potential user should be excluded because of the presentational style employed.

Examples:

- A research team produces a report on autism aimed at parents – is it too long, too dense and too prone to technical language, or is it patronising to the point of insult?
- The Department of Health produces guidelines on charging for the residential care of elderly people – are they clear and unambiguous, comprehensive or selective?

In summary: the basic question to ask of any piece of knowledge is **TAPUPA?**

Transparency – is it open to scrutiny?
Accuracy – is it well grounded?
Purposivity – is it fit for purpose?
Utility – is it fit for use?
Propriety – is it legal and ethical?
Accessibility – is it intelligible?

We forward these criteria as first principles for assessing social care knowledge. They can be employed directly by individual end users of knowledge to help them make judgements about particular documents.

However, it is more likely that they will be used by intermediaries who filter and synthesise the knowledge base on behalf of end users. For example, TAPUPA has considerable potential as a screening framework for information professionals in selecting material for inclusion in bibliographic databases, or creating the more structured, informative abstracts that are increasingly in demand within the social sciences. It could also be of value to systematic reviewers in the social care field where the inclusion/exclusion of material on the basis of strict methodological criteria is often difficult or inappropriate.

It is important to remember that these principles are not intended to be a simple checklist; they do not replace judgement. Experience of their application will be needed to assess their value in practice and identify where they may need amendment, refinement or clarification. Here we offer a brief example, based on a scored assessment of one article by a member of the research team (AL).

An application of TAPUPA

Wenger, G.C. and Tucker, I. (2002) 'Using network variation in practice: identification of support network type', *Health and Social Care in the Community*, vol 10, no 1, pp 28-35.

The aim of this study was to develop an instrument (Practitioner Assessment of Network Type – PANT) to identify support network types for older people, validate it and evaluate its use in social work practice.

Transparency: the study explains its aims, theoretical framework and setting, but needs to provide greater clarity and full details about methods and the process of analysis. However, it would pass 'normal' thresholds on transparency. (Score: 6-7/10)

Accuracy: the findings are credible but no quotes or examples of discussions within meetings are included. Insight into client cases, suitably anonymised, would have added greater depth of insight into the way practitioners used PANT, and how they found it useful for their clients. (Score: 7/10)

Purposivity: the study meets this standard in full. The intervention, sample and modes of fieldwork are appropriate to the purpose of the study. (Score: 10/10)

Utility: the study meets this standard in full insofar as this can be judged by an assessor who is not also the potential end user of this piece of knowledge. The study aims to explore the value, use and acceptability of PANT and achieves this, showing via the experience and views of participating practitioners how it could be of use to others. (Score: 10/10)

Propriety: there is no reason to doubt that this standard was not met. All data are reported in an anonymous form. However, there is no indication as to whether staff were given the option to attend the training, or were required to do so. At the same time, as is common with social care research, the study does not appear to have passed through a Local Research Ethics Committee. Nor is there any statement about how issues of ethics and proper conduct were addressed, save in terms of total confidentiality for client cases. (Score: probably 10/10; met at least partially)

Accessibility: this standard is met. Academic language and jargon is used but this is appropriate for the potential reader and user of an article from an academic, peer reviewed journal.

AL also carried out a parallel assessment of this article using a domain-specific evaluation template for use with qualitative research. Overall, he concludes that:

- TAPUPA is a useful tool because of its breadth of coverage. The study chosen for examination is firmly within the research domain, and the alternative assessment using a domain-specific evaluation template covered many of the TAPUPA elements (transparency, accuracy, purposivity and propriety). However, TAPUPA prompted the additional consideration of important utility and accessibility issues.
- In the other knowledge domains which lack specific quality assessment standards or frameworks of their own, TAPUPA is likely to be much more important.
- The examples appended to each element of TAPUPA help to illustrate the anchor points for judgements and prompt the critical reflection, based on a full and close reading of the article, that is appropriate in a quality assessment context.

This assessment was conducted by a practised researcher with considerable experience of judging the methodological quality of the research literature. For those with similar skills and experience, TAPUPA adds extra dimensions to quality assessment without posing any major technical difficulties. For others who might use this tool – for example information professionals creating records for bibliographic databases – there is likely to be a critical appraisal training requirement. If SCIE intends to employ TAPUPA in this context it will need to consider not only training needs but the inevitable increase in document processing time attendant on the need to read documents critically and in depth.

11.2. Specific standards for different types of knowledge

Important as they are, it is clearly insufficient to rely solely on generic standards. Each piece of knowledge also needs to pass muster in its own field, against the standards operating there. Having identified the diverse sources that comprise social care knowledge, the key ambition of this exercise is to draw together best practice from these contrasting domains. In order to explore similarities and differences, the construction of standards in each domain is followed through the sequence of issues illustrated in Figure 4.

Some of the social care knowledge sources are much more thickly populated with standards than are others and, in many cases, these do not relate directly to the quality assessment of knowledge. The descriptions that follow take into account the future practical use of the framework, and include some preliminary thoughts on how existing (or latent) standards might be adapted for knowledge assessment purposes. Despite the diversity of the knowledge sources, there are certain parallels to be drawn, and reading *across* the five sources can create added value.

Figure 4: **A profile on which to compare standards**

➡ What is covered by the standards?
➡➡ What is the origin of the standards?
➡➡➡ What is the nature of the standards?
➡➡➡➡ How are the standards activated?
➡➡➡➡➡ What is their use and impact?

12

Organisational knowledge

12.1. Coverage

The organisational source is awash with standards governing all aspects of social care including the conduct of organisations and individuals, the regulation of services, and the registration and training of practitioners. Each one subdivides so that there are rules for checking criminal records in staffing, regulations for fire safety in residential homes, requirements for social care workers to prevent self-harm by clients, and so on. The aim is to build a comprehensive accountability framework for all activities in social care.

12.2. Origin

This emphasis on accountability is reflected in the establishment of five bodies to promote and govern standards within the Quality in Social Care national institutional framework[6]. Supplementing these are the Audit Commission and the Social Services Inspectorate (SSI) while, at times of crisis, commissions and inquiries are appointed to reform and fine-tune standards[7]. The standards trail also drives downwards, with regional and local statutory bodies having the power to stipulate and check on standards. Recently, there has been an attempt to weld some of these components together through Joint Reviews of Social Services.

This standards infrastructure has a professional and methodological substance. Standards are buttressed by the authority and training of those who produce and operate them, and whose legitimation is established by a further set of standards for standard-making[8]. These administrative details are rehearsed to show that standards for organisational knowledge are hardened institutionally in a manner that does not apply to standards in the other social care knowledge sources.

12.3. Nature

Organisational standards take on a range of forms but their prime purpose is governance. At their core are regulatory requirements, often in the form of 'minimally acceptable' standards, that cover every aspect of social care practice. For instance in the following extract (one of six sets) from the General Social Care Council (GSCC) *Code of practice for social care workers*[9]:

The regulatory intent of these propositions, which are delivered as a 'must' statement, is evident and there is a clear contrast with the 'should' statements typical of standards in the other four knowledge sources.

Organisational standards also set down clear lines of accountability. An example extracted from the GSCC *Code of practice for employers of social care workers* gives an indication of their nature[10]:

Figure 5: GSCC code of practice for social workers (extract)

As a social care worker you must protect the rights and promote the interests of service users and carers:

This includes:
1.1. Treating each person as an individual.
1.2. Respecting and, where appropriate, promoting the individual views and wishes of both service users and carers.
1.3. Supporting service users' rights to control their lives and make informed choices about the services they receive.
1.4. Respecting and maintaining the dignity and privacy of service users.
1.5. Promoting equal opportunities for service users and carers.
1.6. Respecting diversity and different cultures and values

Other standards in this knowledge source are aspirational and promissory. The imperative changes from 'must' to 'ought' in standards such as the series of *Toolkits* produced by the Leeds Health Authority[11]. A typical format involves: heralding the standard (why do it?), laying down responsibilities (who should do it?), charting courses of action (how to do it?) and measuring outcomes (how to assess it?). Such presumptive standards approach the boundaries of other sources, principally those for practitioner and user knowledge.

Figure 6: GSCC code of practice for employers (extract)

To meet their responsibilities in relation to regulating social care workers, social care employers must:

1.4 Give staff clear information about their roles and responsibilities, relevant legislation and organisational policies and procedures they must follow in their work.
3.2 Contribute to the provision of social care and social work education and training, including effective workplace assessment and practice learning.
4.5 Put in place and implement written policies and procedures that promote staff welfare and equal opportunities.
5.6 Cooperate with GSCC investigations and hearings and respond appropriately to the findings and decisions of the GSCC.

12.4. Activation

Although the organisational domain may seek to enable as well as constrain, many of its standards are safeguarded de facto as statutory rules, regulations and guidance administered through a complex apparatus of training, inspection, audit, inquiry and so on. Because of all this apparatus, organisational standards are often thought of as 'given' – they cannot be challenged, and so 'write themselves' into the chapter and verse of practice.

In reality there is a range of reasons why the organisational knowledge embodied in standards is not simply 'given'. Factors such as risk aversion[12] or resistance[13] can subvert the 'writing in' process, while the notion of standards as something simply handed down to a subordinate body for implementation has been overtaken by 'the revolution in accountability'. The 'modernisation' of government has led to a proliferation of standard making processes but, crucially, these now involve attempts to involve a wider range of stakeholders[14].

The recognition that standards do not simply fall into place has also led to an extended role for the bodies that check and maintain them. Auditors no longer just check that the books balance, and the concern of inspectors goes well beyond probity. Evaluative standards are being created around much more difficult issues such as, 'do interventions work?', 'are authorities providing best value?', and 'do services interlink properly?'[15]. One fruit of these changes are the standards applied in Joint Reviews, and the following quotation captures the upgraded notion of 'reality checking', including the link into other knowledge sources and the borrowing of some of their standards apparatus.

> Reviewers draw upon a social scientific methodology in a pragmatic and eclectic manner – this includes documentary analysis of, and in respect of, policies and plans; comparative statistical analysis of cost and service data: surveys, focus groups and home visits with selective users and carers; individual and group interviews with staff from local authorities and agencies which provide social care; visits to day centres, residential centres and special projects, etc. The methodological innovation resides in the strategy of 'reality checking' which sutures together the multiple methods[16].

12.5. Use and impact

Organisational standards have a quite different scope and significance from those operating in other domains of social care. While many of these are, so to speak, waiting in the wings, organisational standards of considerable depth and coverage already prevail. SCIE is sister to the GSCC and insofar as SCIE is committed to discovering best practice in those social care activities embedded within statutory and regulatory standards, there is a clear case for making use of the GSCC framework.

SCIE is seeking criteria on which to judge knowledge from all five sources identified in Figure 3 and it is quite possible that subsets of the GSCC codes could be used as the basis of appraising knowledge outside the purely organisational domain. For instance, Figure 5 provides an embryonic set of issues on which to evaluate knowledge involving the rights of users and carers. For use as appraisal instruments the GSCC codes would have to be treated as more than 'minimal standards', and perhaps elaborated with further indicators and exemplars. Nevertheless, their coverage is so wide that the adaptation of quality standards from the national institutional framework remains a key starting point for knowledge standards. Given further refinement, the more aspirational standards produced within the organisational sphere also hold promise as tools for knowledge appraisal.

Practitioner knowledge

13.1. Coverage

The literature searches did not uncover any explicit standards to appraise practitioner knowledge. As this is commonly tacit, passed on through word of mouth and observation, the notion of explicit rules for its quality assessment may seem a contradiction in terms. At the same time, everyday experience is widely reported and reflected on in print for the benefit of the wider social care community, for example in practitioner journals. It is also documented in reports of good and best practice, especially in guidance and other documents arising from the organisational and policy knowledge sources.

13.2. Origin

Practitioner knowledge is acquired directly through the practice of social caring and the distillation of collective wisdom at many points through media such as education and training, requesting and receiving advice, attending team meetings and case conferences, and comparing notes. It is from these cooperative encounters, especially the more formal ones, that it may be possible to derive some elemental quality standards. Further codification may arise from working with practitioners to assist them in making explicit how they arrive at decisions.

13.3. Nature

Practitioner knowledge belongs to the personal dimension, and distilling everyday experience is not simple. On the one hand it is the raison d'être for a personal approach to social care in which practitioners "judge their efforts in terms of emotional rewards, peer approval, lack of harm caused, client appreciation, and gut reactions that 'the case is moving on'"[17]. On the other hand "social workers' widespread preference for a personal, private style of working is a major obstacle to changing their use of theories and evaluating practice"[18].

Where practitioner knowledge is written and explicit, quality standards might appropriately be drawn and adapted from within the research knowledge domain and particularly from the qualitative research style[19]. These include:

- The authenticity and credibility of the source (who is the practitioner, what is their experience, what is their contact with the context and setting reported on?).
- The credibility of the content, including evidence of traceable links to practice.
- The provision of sufficient detail for wider relevance and take-up into others' practice.

At an elemental level, the core of a quality standard for tacit practitioner knowledge is a retrospective assessment of the correctness of the decision-making process and implemented actions arising for a social care practitioner in his/her everyday work. Two strands of research are evident in the literature, both of which attempt to articulate formally and explicitly how, and why, particular decisions are reached: reflection on practice; and 'mining' or articulating the unspoken.

The idea of reflective practice lies at the heart of practitioner knowledge[20]. In action learning sets[21], participants work together to share experiences and reflections on action, providing constructive comments, advice, and ideas on future action. In 'peer reflection schemes' practitioner teams, backed by facilitators and administrative support, reflect systematically on common issues pertinent to their work with clients. As part of this process prior intuitions and experiences may become hardened into written action plans, providing a format to codify the knowledge and then arrive at quality standards.

Mining engages practitioners in a research process that involves 'articulating the unspoken'. In the context of this exercise, interest lies in the way that this articulation may uncover implicit standards for the knowledge itself. In one approach, Rosen and colleagues[22] disinter and decipher case records produced by social workers in their assessment, intervention and referral of a class of clients presenting with the same problem. The practitioners employ a standard grid for making detailed case notes that spells out the stages in decision making and documents a 'personal logic of intervention'. Each decision tree is then coded for similarities and differences. A large sample of such records enables mapping of the typical and preferred patterns of intervention.

Sheppard and colleagues[23] pursue a slightly different approach, presenting social workers with case 'vignettes'. Participants are then asked to 'think aloud' about the procedures and protocols they would employ in dealing with the case. Using a sample of social workers, each working through the same scenario, provides the opportunity to investigate the patterning of practitioner knowledge.

These two strands of research illustrate embryonic standards of a rather different sort. From the field of action learning, one may derive standards for an institutional framework required to marshal practitioner knowledge. This may involve requirements for regular time away from practice areas, support of a facilitator, mutual trust and confidentiality, and the production of action and implementation plans[24]. From research aimed at 'articulating the unspoken' insight is provided into the concealed formal structure of practitioner knowledge. Standards may then involve the credibility of the alternative hypotheses developed, the critical appraisal process and the choice of 'if, then' statements about prospective practice actions. Both of these approaches are 'hot topics' in social care training. For example, Morrison and Horwarth's recommendations echo the action learning approach by proposing a standard relating to learning partnerships[25], while the decision logic unearthed by the 'mining studies' bears a strong family resemblance to the critical thinking advocated by Gambrill[26].

13.4. Activation

The 'activation' phase of Figure 4 relates to the decision by a group of stakeholders to take up an agreed set of standards, apply and implement them. This phase seems to be entirely absent from practitioner knowledge since much of this is unrecorded and unstandardised. However, one reason why such knowledge exerts so powerful an influence, and appropriately stands shoulder to shoulder with the other sources of knowledge in Figure 3, is because it brims with *latent* standards. Thus while evidence based practice pre-supposes a rational decision making model (choice between explicit alternative interventions, each with an associated probability of success), in the tacit model, practitioners may make selective observations on a case, and then go through a personal and experientially based archive of patterns and experiences to arrive at a chosen course of action.

13.5. Use and impact

The mining studies suggest that practitioner knowledge operates through a highly analytical and critical process. This process awareness provides a potential basis for standards in this knowledge domain. As Sheppard et al comment, "the data presented here ... represent the beginnings of the means by which we can evaluate minimal standards of practice, and develop ways of educating social workers for these minimum standards (or better)"[27]. Zeira and Rosen concur, perceiving in their research on tacit knowledge the possibility of producing guidelines on how to appraise the alternative hypotheses that gather around a particular class of intervention targets[28].

Appraising the quality of 'tales from the field' could take the form of making judgements on the basis of evidence of some collective heart-searching in their production. For example, do they bear the marks of approved, regular, confidential, supported, collective time for reflection? Alternatively, the critical thinking formulas could be applied. For example, do the accounts reflect information scrutiny, hypothesis development, selection between courses of action, staged strategy development, and so on?

Joyce points out that it is a fairly short step from 'action learning groups' to 'action research teams' and to 'research awareness associations'[29]. Instead of 'figuring out best practice' their core activities would be, respectively, 'testing out best practice' and 'seeking out best practice'. Standards appropriate to these missions may be considered to fall under the research knowledge umbrella. This is one of several examples of the mutual benefit gained by borrowing from standards regimes across knowledge sources.

14

Policy community knowledge

14.1. Coverage

This source provides vital knowledge about how social care does, might or should fit into its complex political, social and economic environment. It is also among the most thinly populated with formal standards although many contributors assert criteria for best practice in policy making. Policy community knowledge ranges from the profession of broad principles to underpin social services (for example, from 'welfare to well-being'), to suggestions for structural models to deliver them (for example, 'public–private partnerships'), to the promotion of implementation strategies (for example, 'user and carer involvement'). It is often rhetorical or speculative: "As politicians know only too well, but social scientists too often forget, public policy is made of language. Whether in written or oral form, argumentation is central to all stages of the policy process"[30].

14.2. Origin

The key contributors to policy community knowledge include officials of central, regional and local government and its agencies, the members of think tanks and lobby groups, policy and research staff in political parties and their affiliates, and scholars of public policy. Their outputs range from newspaper and magazine articles to pamphlets and reports ('grey' literature), official documents (especially Green and White Papers), and academic journal papers and books. The sources with the greatest potential in a search for knowledge standards are analytical and reflective pieces on policy making which consider the optimal forms of its components such as formation, drafting and implementation.

14.3. Nature

This is not an area in which standards are presented as formal frameworks. Quality principles are more likely to surface as general 'markers', 'concepts' and 'competencies'. They suggest ways that things could be done better, and the potential sources of improvement, rather than providing a detailed blueprint of best practice. As such they tend to be aspirational and promotional, reflecting the rhetorical and argumentative nature of this particular knowledge source.

This presents a dilemma for the would-be standards maker and it is necessary to re-state a point made in Chapter 10, namely that some forms of knowledge, especially ideological and political reasoning, can never be appraised against a quality criterion. Accordingly, the search for standards is restricted to that portion of policy community knowledge that claims to forward testable claims about policy making, rather than asserting ideological preferences for policy choices. This is emphatically *not* to say that other kinds of policy community outputs should be dismissed by the knowledge seeker. The speculative or rhetorical can have great value (depending on information need) even if it falls at every formal quality appraisal fence. Indeed, freedom from the constraining requirement to be strictly evidence based and testable may be a sine qua non of the most innovatory and profound thinking.

Given the dearth of agreed standards in this area any recommendations must necessarily take the form of a speculative journey, in this case using as an example the Cabinet Office report on *Better policy making*[31] which is one element of the government's wider attempt to develop a model of 'modernised and professional policy-making'[32]. If its general standards have veracity, then their form (if not content) might be adapted for the social care context and for the quality assessment of policy community knowledge.

Better policy making argues that knowledge should be useful and relevant to policy makers, helping them to be forward looking and to demonstrate foresight and connectivity. Its key feature is the identification of nine core 'competencies' or standards that are argued to encapsulate the key elements of the modern policy-making process.

Figure 7: **A taxonomy of standards for policy making**

i) Forward looking
ii) Outward looking
iii) Innovative, flexible and creative
iv) Evidence-based
v) Inclusive
vi) Joined up
vii) Subject to review
viii) Evaluated
ix) Lesson learning

Figure 8: **Some key markers of forward and outward looking policy**

- Early identification of outcomes and a communication strategy to present them
- Using contingency or scenario planning (to identify unintended consequences and cross-domain effects
- Bringing in people from outside into policy teams
- Looking at the experience of national and regional variation and how other countries do things

Some of these standards are reflected in other knowledge sources; for example, the call for evidence-based inquiry is also characteristic of the research community. However, those concerned with promoting skills and thinking are especially characteristic of this knowledge source. For each of the competencies, there are further markers to demonstrate that the objective in question has been met. For example, and quite uniquely, there is an attempt to set standards for 'thinking outside the box'.

14.4. Activation

The status of these standards is clearly provisional. *Better policy making* goes on to identify the 'drivers', 'benefits', 'barriers', and 'enablers' that surround the implementation of a new approach to policy making. Key drivers originate in senior government ranks and in the need to maintain the civil service at the forefront of policy making. Key benefits cluster round broad concurrence with the aims of the modernising government agenda. Key barriers include the limitations imposed on changing practice by tight timetables, hierarchical structures, a risk-averse culture and lack of training. Key enablers include improved sharing of best practice and a higher profile for implementation issues in the policy maker's brief.

Even in this most conjectural area, there are the beginnings of a standards framework. In particular, *Better policy making* and related documents in the 'modernising government' canon use a similar expository structure on standards to that employed in more mature fields of quality assurance[33]. The identification of 'competencies' and their 'key markers' is akin to the shift from 'principles' to 'indicators', while the use of wide-ranging examples of 'good practice' is again customary in establishing a standards framework. In activating such a framework 'peer review' is a well-established mechanism, and this has been introduced in the Cabinet Office as part of the drive for better policy making, alongside other quality-promoting initiatives such as knowledge pools[34].

14.5. Usage

There is a long and perhaps insurmountable hill to climb before standard setting and application become priority issues in the policy community. The *Better policy making* framework describes the key competencies as 'features' rather than standards, and there is no formal apparatus to quality check emerging policies against them. However, as 'aspirations', it seems not unreasonable to claim that such 'features' have the potential to inspire and promote change.

When it comes to the assessment of documented policy community knowledge, it is possible that markers such as those highlighted in Figures 7 and 8 could be used as the basis of quality standards. More research is clearly needed on knowledge quality standards in this domain but the *Better policy making* example has at least provided some initial tools for promoting greater transparency in the assessment and use of policy knowledge. In addition, useful insights into its quality can be gained by applying the generic standards proposed in Chapter 11.

Research community knowledge

15.1. Coverage

Standards abound in the research knowledge domain. It is an area that members of the research community both talk and write about and one that is undergoing continual elaboration and refinement. Recognised and accepted standards, presented in the form of methodological questions, checklists and evaluative frameworks, are increasingly available for the multiple families of research strategies. Examples include: RCTs[35]; action research[36]; economic evaluation[37]; qualitative research designs[38]; and methods for systematic review within the Cochrane[39] and Campbell Collaborations[40].

15.2. Origin

Quality standards in the research community are rooted in debates about what counts as knowledge and truth. Standards have been generated through and in relation to peer reference groups within particular disciplines, across disciplines, and within and across research approaches. There are a variety of forms including peer review of grant proposals and publications; professional standards for research within particular disciplines (emanating, for example, from the British Sociological Association, Social Research Association, UK Evaluation Society, and Social Sciences Research Group[41]); and external evaluation of the research community through, for example, the higher education funding councils' Research Assessment Exercise. The standards themselves are inculcated through academic research education and training across the qualification spectrum, and through the process of doing research.

15.3. Nature

Debates about quality standards for research knowledge take the form of discussions in three areas: research design, research practice and, more recently, the take-up of research into practice. The main body of work focuses on research design, in particular:

- What counts as 'high' quality research, in general?
- What research designs are most appropriate to particular sorts of research question? For example, the RCT for questions of cause and effect, and qualitative research using observation and interviewing to understand process features or to capture the meanings of participants.
- How can the quality of particular research designs be assessed? Design is variously interpreted as referring to the design as such, and/or doing the research and/or the (potential for) take-up of research into practice.

These core questions are answered by reference to many of the generic principles outlined in Chapter 11, in particular transparency, accuracy, purposivity and propriety. These principles are related to general features of research, for example, informed consent, the balance of doing good and doing harm, control of sources of bias and potential for generalisability. Of central concern is the principle of openness of method, or the provision of adequate details about how the study was done to allow it to be replicated, or for its findings to be taken up in practice. More recently, with the promotion of evidence-based practice, the principle of 'relevance' or 'utility' has come more to the fore, focusing on the relevance of the research question and research findings to practice or policy.

These principles are commonly translated into a set of methodological questions and/or checklists, to be applied to written reports on the design and undertaking of research. Sometimes the checklists are of a general form (that is, drawing on elements that make for high quality of research). In other instances, the questions relate directly to the nature of a particular research style (for example, qualitative or quantitative). The decision made is explicitly a judgement over quality. Good practice involves the appraiser making explicit why a particular judgement is reached, for example, the chain of reasoning that led to doubts over sample size or data interpretation as severely affecting the wider validity of the study and its conclusions.

15.4. Activation

While there are elements of commonality in standards frameworks (for example, clarity of the research question, fitness of the particular research study to the research question, adoption of ethical practices), there are also points of difference relating to the underlying approach of the research design. In addition, evaluating the quality of research is not uncontested. Some query the validity and usefulness of this process noting, for example, that: doing research is messy; reports are only accounts of how the research was done; and page limits in journals and books reduce the amount of space that can be devoted to how a study was done. Others question the appropriateness of the evaluation activity per se. This is most notable within the qualitative style where some argue that the reflexivity and relativity of qualitative inquiry mean that it is irrelevant and inappropriate to develop criteria to judge its products[42]. Finally, there is debate over the priority or relative importance of the multiple components of the methodological questions/checklists.

There has also been debate about the ability of essentially self-regulatory structures for appraisal and review to promote good quality research. Following the emergence of a number of high profile ethical scandals, the Department of Health has established a research governance framework for health and social care[43]. This outlines principles of good research practice, elaborates the responsibilities and accountabilities of all parties, and introduces a monitoring and inspection system. Key responsibilities for researchers relate to the areas of employer approval for research to take place, research ethics committee approval, and informed consent.

At present, the framework plays a 'gatekeeping' and 'forward looking' monitoring role. Proposed research that does not come up to standard will not be allowed to go forward; access to settings will be denied, and permission to do the research withheld. Responsibility to ensure adherence to the principle of propriety falls to the researcher's employer organisation and the research sponsor. The Department of Health is monitoring the degree of compliance within NHS organisations via a baseline assessment, while arrangements for social care are being developed as part of the implementation of the quality framework for social care[44]. The Social Services Research Group supports the implementation of the research governance framework across social care, "so that it enhances the quality and ethical standards of research in a practical and realistic way"[45]. However, issues of ethics and quality are often confused, and it is notable that there are currently few, if any, arrangements for seeking ethical approval within social care.

15.5. Use and impact

The various evaluation tools and checklists are in routine use within the systematic review industry and in any context where the critical appraisal of research is either central or highly rewarded. The latter include the promotion of evidence-based practice, with its emphasis on all research users being able to judge the quality of a piece of research. Such tools could, with benefit, be used more systematically and thoroughly to guide research design and to judge its quality.

It can be argued that the use of standards has affected the quality of research in two significant ways. Firstly, despite journal article limitations, more recently published articles give more detail about the way studies are done, and about the meaning of such terms as 'grounded theory', 'thematic analysis' and 'randomised into groups'. Secondly, critical appraisal is now routinely taught within academic training at undergraduate and postgraduate level, and is likely to become a core competency within continuing professional development in social care and elsewhere.

Despite the abundance and widespread usage of standards, judging the quality of research knowledge is still not without difficulty. The very abundance of standards generates problems of choice, perhaps suggesting that these also need to be subjected to quality appraisal. There are also limited guarantees that standards are followed. Implementation can be weak or permissive, for example in the context of publication peer review[46], while the effect on research practice is rarely evaluated. The impact of the research governance framework, in particular, deserves close attention.

User and carer knowledge

16.1. Coverage

The growth of user and carer-oriented initiatives has marked a sea change in the provision of social care in the last decade. These comprise a movement with a range of different ambitions, ranging from 'giving users a voice' to 'increasing user participation' to 'ceding to user control'[47]. In addition there are parallel, and sometimes overlapping, movements within the organisational and policy communities in which user and carer knowledge is considered as part of the debate about democratic accountability in which emerging standards about consultation and participation play a major role. Within the user and carer community itself, examples of emerging standards can be found in user-led and emancipatory research[48], and the activities and publications of user organisations such as the British Council of Disabled People[49].

16.2. Origin

The source of these standards lies within user and carer organisations, and they have developed within a political movement centred on 'giving users a voice'. They have also been informed by the involvement of those with research expertise, who are either themselves users or carers or empathetic to the importance of the 'active consumer' view. They perceive research knowledge as part of a way to articulate a legitimate and but under-recognised voice.

16.3. Nature

Standards in this area are essentially aspirational. They set out criteria which user and carer knowledge 'should' meet and, particularly in the organisational arena, which social care services 'should' meet. They revolve around the twin principles of 'participation' and 'accountability'. Participation connects to the wisdom of users and carers ('it's time to listen to people who know') and centres on an insistence about who should control research. Accountability centres on the need for all aspects of the conceptualisation, development, implementation, management and evaluation of services to be in the hands of users. This is translated into the knowledge generation process through accountability to user groups and their membership.

Standards for user and carer knowledge are emergent, with many statements of first principles that draw on examples of best practice. For example, drawing on a 'disability' and 'emancipatory' research perspective[50], high quality user and carer knowledge should be able to demonstrate the following:

- *Accountability:* all knowledge production should be answerable to social care users and their organisations.
- *Use of a 'social model':* all knowledge should adhere to an explanatory model, focusing on the institutional, economic, environmental and cultural barriers – and their social and psychological consequences – for disadvantaged groups and individuals.
- *Clarity of ideological standpoint:* as all knowledge is coloured by the political complexion of its producers, there should be a clear declaration of loyalties.
- *Empowerment:* all knowledge should be judged on whether it has meaningful political and practical outcomes for users, rather than simply being assessed on paper.

The principle of participation may be taken forward in terms of mapping the types of user and carer participation (passive, consultative, active and ownership) against the various phases of the research process, from problem identification and design to writing up, dissemination and action[51]. The core idea of such an evaluative grid (Figure 9), produced in a project commissioned by the Empowerment Sub-group of Consumers in the NHS, is that the user orientation should infuse every stage of the research process.

Figure 9: **Levels of participation at different stages of the research cycle**

Type of user participation				
Project cycle	Passive	Consul-tative	Active	Ownership
Problem identification				
Project design				
Planning				
Data collection				
Data analysis				
Writing up				
Dissemination				
Action and evaluation				

Good practice is reflected in research in which the majority of elements are judged to fall into the active and ownership types of participation. This and other grids can be deepened using a further range of modifications, such as the production of advice and examples ('tips of the trade') about how to achieve the ownership goal at each stage.

There are, however, significant differences of opinion on what constitutes the 'gold standard' of participation. Debate centres on the extent to which best practice involves the search for 'user control,' or a 'full/equal partnership' between users and practitioners[52].

The principle of accountability may be taken forward by identifying key features of best practice in user-controlled organisations, including:

- the wish to bring about radical change;
- recruitment practices designed to employ 'people like those using the services';
- using a social model to plan access to and the nature of services;
- flexibility in the delivery of services to respond to the varied need of users;

- increasing users' choice and their control over their own lives;
- involving users in all decisions about the delivery of services.

Looking beyond the core principles of participation and accountability, there is also debate over whether quality criteria appropriate to the production of user and carer knowledge should be adopted or adapted from the research community. A limited consultation with a range of user and carer groups, undertaken as part of this project, suggests agreement with the notion that the standards appropriate to user-led research should be no different from the standards that are applicable to research conducted by 'professionals'.

16.4. Activation

Standards are realised through the ongoing work and activities of user and carer organisations but it is not known to what extent they are followed through. They are beginning to permeate across to other knowledge sources, for example, research[53] and, most significantly, organisational knowledge.

For the former, the increasing advocacy of user involvement by sponsors requires the research community to address its form, extent and stages of occurrence. There is also a growing understanding of the need to develop outcome indicators and measures that give priority to user and carer perspectives. This leads on to a concern with the importance of exploring the experiences of users and carers in order both to understand the nature of the intervention process, and to explore the cause-effect link.

From the 'organisational' perspective, a similar shift in perspective is underway. The concern here is with implementing the accountability principle and evaluating its execution. Thus Best Value performance reviews combine the measurement of service performance with the idea of accountability to local citizens[54].

16.5. Use and impact

The various grids of participation are commonly used by user organisations as an aid to development and progress-chasing in service provision, and by members of the research community to produce more user-friendly research. They may also be used post hoc as a means of evaluating the quality of documented accounts of completed research.

Despite burgeoning interest in standards issues within this knowledge domain, little is known so far about their likely impact. However, the chances of consensus on what constitutes quality may be slim given the existence of stakeholder groups with very different aims and objectives. Those who are concerned with greater user involvement in service planning and delivery, for example, are likely to have very different priorities from those who seek to challenge 'anti-oppressive practice'[55].

17

Conclusion

This report has outlined a framework for assessing the quality of social care knowledge within five source domains. It is based around a set of six generic standards or principles operating across the domains, and standards or principles that apply (or might be adapted for application) within each of the domains. The latter suggest the addition of a seventh generic standard, namely specificity: does the knowledge pass muster within its own domain, as perceived by its participants and proponents? The basic question to be asked of any piece of knowledge thus becomes **TAPUPAS?**

Transparency – is it open to scrutiny?
Accuracy – is it well grounded?
Purposivity – is it fit for purpose?
Utility – is it fit for use?
Propriety – is it legal and ethical?
Accessibility – is it intelligible?
Specificity – does it meet source-specific standards?

Phrasing standards in this way makes clear that they do not replace judgement. They are part of an appraisal process, providing a reference point for judgements and a context against which to explain why and how judgements are made. To use the framework appropriately, a user must therefore state how the piece of knowledge has, or has not, met the standards. It is as important to know why one piece of knowledge is accepted or included as to know why another is rejected and excluded. The generic standards offer a coherent and rational approach to judging the quality of evidence from all five knowledge sources. Although requiring considerable further refinement in the light of experience with their application, they are likely to figure prominently in SCIE's initial development of the knowledge quality framework. Important in their own right, they currently offer a practical way forward for assessing quality from those knowledge sources where specific standards remain emergent, latent or inappropriate. Figure 10 summarises the very mixed state of play across the sources.

An important message to emerge from this analysis is the interweaving of different sources in standards development. Potential standards for practitioner knowledge are emerging from the research domain. The principle of participation has permeated from the user and carer across to the organisational and research domains. Organisational standards for research governance are being imposed on researchers while some of their standards (for example, in relation to critical appraisal) are attracting interest within government. In developing knowledge appraisal standards, there is scope not just for adapting standards developed for other purposes within a particular domain, but also for borrowing standards from other domains.

This report is a foundation point for exploring a complex world of latent, emerging and actual standards that might be applied to knowledge. The model to be used should be one of 'apply … refine … apply … re-refine' in an ongoing development spiral which focuses on improving the robustness of standards and their intelligibility, practicality and acceptability to a wide range of social care knowledge users.

Figure 10: Standards: the state of play

	Source 1 Organisational knowledge	Source 2 Practitioner knowledge	Source 3 Policy community knowledge	Source 4 Research knowledge	Source 5 User and carer knowledge
Coverage	All social care activities	Minimal. Potentially applicable only to documented knowledge	Minimal. Potentially applicable only to part of the knowledge base	All social research perspectives	Minimal
Nature	Rules, regulations, codes of practice, statutory and aspirational guidance	Latent within the process of practitioner decision making	Emergent. Concepts, competencies, markers of good practice rather than formal standards	Abundant sets of methodological rules	Emergent. Rooted in demands for accountability and participation

cont .../

Figure 10: contd.../

	Source 1 Organisational knowledge	Source 2 Practitioner knowledge	Source 3 Policy community knowledge	Source 4 Research knowledge	Source 5 User and carer knowledge
Origin	Within the organisational domain at national, regional and local level; increasing external involvement through consultation processes	Potential development from analysis of reflective practice by researchers working with practitioners; and from qualitative research standards	Organisational domain at present but, potentially, also from think tanks, political parties, public policy scholars	Largely within the research domain; involvement of government departments and agencies in recent years	Potential development by multiple sources: user/carer bodies; research domain; policy community; government

cont .../

Figure 10: contd.../

	Source 1 Organisational knowledge	Source 2 Practitioner knowledge	Source 3 Policy community knowledge	Source 4 Research knowledge	Source 5 User and carer knowledge
Activation	Statutory implementation, inspection and audit	Unknown	Unknown	Internal self-regulation; recent introduction of external monitoring and inspection	Unknown
Use and impact	Use imposed by statute; adherence or avoidance	Unknown	Unknown	Routinely used, implementation sometimes weak, impact largely unknown	Unknown

References

1   Barnes, C. (2002) *Types and quality of knowledge seminar: Searching for standards* (available in hard copy: e-mail a.l.boaz@qmul.ac.uk).

2   Grayson, L. (2002) *Social care knowledge: A 'fit for purpose' classification*, Published as ESRC UK Centre for Evidence-based Policy and Practice Working Paper 14, available via http://www.evidencenetwork.org

3   Pawson, R. et al (November 2002) *Types and quality of social care knowledge: Stage One: A classification of types of social care knowledge*, Report to SCIE. (For three background papers, see: Pawson, R. (2003) *Social care knowledge: Seeing the wood for the trees*; Pawson, R. (2003) *Social care knowledge: SCIE-like 'typologies'*; and Grayson, L. (2003) *Social care knowledge: A 'fit for purpose classification*. They are available as Numbers 12-14 in the ESRC UK Centre for Evidence-based Policy and Practice Working Paper series via http://www.evidencenetwork.org.)

4   This work is documented in detail in: Pawson, R. *Shifting standards: Towards a quality framework for social care*, available in the ESRC UK Centre for Evidence-based Policy and Practice Working Paper series via http://www.evidencenetwork.org

5   We deliberately avoid the use of predetermined definitions of certain key terms and occasionally use 'evidence' and 'knowledge' interchangeably. *Evidence* is usually thought of as the empirical means that support more abstract and theoretical forms of *knowledge*, and it can also undergird *practical decisions* (as embodied in the phrase 'evidence-based policy'). However, it is not always easy to maintain strict distinctions; for example, in social care there is a school of thought which perceives practical knowledge as the empirical evidence that can guide more general theory. The boundaries between the practical, the empirical and the theoretical are always in a state of flux, and our terminology reflects this.

6   These bodies are the National Care Standards Commission; TOPSS; the General Social Care Council; the Social Services Inspectorate; and the Social Care Institute for Excellence.

[7]   The Climbié Inquiry (http://www.victoria-climbie-inquiry.org.uk) is just the latest of these.

[8]   For example, Social Services Inspectorate, and Joint Review Team (2002) *Getting the best from Best value: Sharing the experience of applying best value in social care*, London: Department of Health. Available via http://www.doh.gov.uk/ssi/gettingbestvalue.htm; and Hopkins, G. (2000) *An inspector calls: A practical look at social care inspection*, Lyme Regis: Russell House.

[9]   GSCC's *Code of practice for social care workers*, available via http://www.gscc.org.uk/codes_practice.htm

[10]   GSCC's *Code of practice for employers of social care workers*, available via http://www.gscc.org.uk/code_practice.htm

[11]   *Toolkits* have been produced on partnership self-assessment, project evaluation, project planning, project implementation, communications, and service user and carer involvement. They are available via http://www.haznet.org.uk

[12]   Clark, A. and Oswald, A. (1996) *Status risk-aversion and following behaviour in social and economic settings*, The Warwick Economic Research Paper Series, No 476, Coventry: Department of Economics, Warwick University.

[13]   Cragg, M. (1997) 'Performance indicators in the public sector: evidence from the Job Training Partnership', Act *Journal of Law, Economics and Organization*, vol 13, no 1, pp 147-68.

[14]   Cabinet Office (1999) *Modernising government*, Cm 4310, London: The Stationery Office, available via http://www.archive.official-documents.co.uk/document/cm43/4310/4310.htm

[15]   Humphrey, J. (2002) 'A scientific approach to politics? On the trail of the Audit Commission', *Critical Perspectives on Accounting*, vol 13, no 1, pp 39-62.

[16] Humphrey, J. (2002) 'Joint Reviews: retracing the trajectory, decoding the terms', *British Journal of Social Work*, vol 32, no 4, pp 463-76.

[17] Shaw, I. and Shaw, A. (1997) 'Game plans, buzzes, and sheer luck: doing well in social work', *Social Work Research*, vol 21, no 2, pp 69-79.

[18] Munro, E. (1998) 'Improving social workers' knowledge base in child protection work', *British Journal of Social Work*, vol 28, no 1, pp 89-106.

[19] Hammersley, M. (1998) *Reading ethnographic research: A critical guide* (2nd edn), London: Longman.

[20] Schön, D. (1983) *The reflective practitioner: How professionals think in action*, New York, NY: Basic Books.

[21] Revans, R.W. (1980) *Action learning: New techniques for management*, London: Blond and Briggs.

[22] Rosen, A., Proctor, E. and Staudt, M. (1999) 'Social work research and the quest for effective practice', *Social Work Research*, vol 23, no 1, pp 4-14.

[23] Sheppard, M., Newstead, S., di Caccavo, A. and Ryan, K. (2000) 'Reflexivity and the development of process knowledge in social work', *British Journal of Social Work*, vol 30, no 4, pp 465-88; Sheppard, M., Newstead, S., di Caccavo, A. and Ryan, K. (2000) 'Comparative hypothesis assessment and quasi-triangulation as process assessment strategies in social work practice', *British Journal of Social Work*, vol 31, no 6, pp 863-85.

[24] For example, see Joyce, L. (1999) 'Development of practice', in S. Hamer and G. Collinson, *Achieving evidence-based practice*, London: Baillière Tindall.

[25] Morrison, T. and Horwath, J. (1999) *Effective staff training in social care: From theory to practice*, London: Routledge.

[26] Gambrill, E. (200) 'The role of critical thinking in evidence-based social work', in P. Allen-Meares and C. Garvin (eds) *The handbook of social work direct practice*, Thousand Oaks, CA: Sage Publications, pp 43-63.

[27] Sheppard, M., Newstead, S., di Caccavo, A. and Ryan, K. (2000) 'Reflexivity and the development of process knowledge in social work', *British Journal of Social Work*, vol 30, no 4, p 482.

[28] Zeira, A. and Rosen, A. (2000) 'Unravelling "tacit knowledge": what social workers do and why they do it', *Social Services Review*, vol 74, no 1, pp 103-23.

[29] Op cit footnote 17.

[30] Majone, G. (1989) *Evidence, argument and persuasion in the policy process*, New Haven, CT: Yale University Press.

[31] Bullock, H., Mountford, J. and Stanley, R. (2001) *Better policy making*, London: Cabinet Office Centre for Management and Policy Studies, available at http://www.cmps.gov.uk/better_policy_making.pdf

[32] Wyatt, A. (2002) 'Evidence based policy making: the view from a centre', *Public Policy and Administration*, vol 17, no 3, pp 12-28 (this provides a useful summary and review of *Better policy making* and associated reports).

[33] For example, the Joint Committee on Standards for Educational Evaluation (1994) *The program evaluation standards* (2nd edn), Thousand Oaks, CA: Sage Publications.

[34] See: National Audit Office (2001) *Modern policy-making: Ensuring policies deliver value for money*, HC 289, London: The Stationery Office, available at http://www.nao.gov.uk/publications/nao_reports/01-02/0102289.pdf

[35] For example, Moher, D., Schulz, K.F., Altman, D.G. and Lepage, L. for the CONSORT Group (2001) 'The CONSORT statement: revised recommendations for improving the quality of reports of parallel-group randomized trials', *Lancet*, vol 357, no 9263, pp 1190-4.

[36] For example, Waterman, H., Tillen, D., Dickson, R. and de Konig, K. (2001) 'Action research: a systematic review and guidance for assessment', *Health Technology Assessment*, vol 5, no 23, available at http://www.ncchta.org/fullmono/mon523.pdf

37   For example, Drummond, M.F. and Jefferson, T. (1996) 'Guidelines for authors and peer reviewers of economic submissions to the BMJ', *British Medical Journal*, vol 313, no 7052, pp 275-83.

38   For example, Murphy, E., Dingwall, R., Greatbatch, D., Parker, S. and Watson, P. (1998) 'Qualitative research methods in health technology assessment: a review of the literature', *Health Technology Assessment*, vol 2, no 16, available at http://www.hta.nhsweb.nhs.uk/fullmono/mono216.pdf; and Spencer, L., Ritchie, J., Lewis, J. and Dillon, L. (forthcoming) *Assessing quality in qualitative evaluations*, London: National Centre for Social Research.

39   Cochrane Collaboration, http://www.update-software.com/collaboration

40   Campbell Collaboration, http://www.campbellcollaboration.org

41   Respectively to be found via http://www.britsoc.org.uk, http://www.the-sra-org.uk, http://evaluation.org.uk and http://www.ssrg.org.uk

42   Smith, J. (1984) 'The problem of criteria for judging interpretive inquiry', *Educational Evaluation and Policy Analysis*, vol 6, pp 379-91.

43   Department of Health (2001) *Research governance framework for health and social care*, London: Department of Health, available via http://www.doh.gov.uk/research/documents/listofpublications.htm

44   Department of Health2000) *A quality strategy for social care*, London: Department of Health, available at http://www.doh.gov.uk/pdfs/qstrategy.pdf

45   Social Sciences Research Group (2003) *Current consultations*, www.ssrg.org.uk/briefins/consult/govern2.htm, accessed 12 February 2003.

46   For example, Grayson, L. *Evidence based policy and the quality of evidence: Rethinking peer review*, Working Paper 7, London: ESRC UK Centre for Evidence-based Policy and Practice, available via http://www.evidencenetwork.org

[47] Arnstein, S. (1996) 'A ladder of citizen participation', *Journal of the American Institute of Planners*, vol 35, no 4, pp 216-24.

[48] For example, Barnes, M., Harrison, S.J., Mort, M. and Shardlow, P. (1999) *Unequal partners: User groups and community care*, Bristol: The Policy Press; Goodley, D. (2000) *Self-advocacy in the lives of people with learning disabilities: The politics of resilience*, Buckingham: Open University Press.

[49] *Personal Assistance Users' Newsletter*, available via http://www.ncil.org.uk/newsletters.asp; see also publications of the Creating Independent Futures initiative at http://www.leeds.ac.uk/disability-studies/projects/independentfutures.htm

[50] Barnes, C. (2003) 'What a difference a decade makes: reflections on doing "emancipatory" disability research', *Disability and Society*, vol 18, no 1, pp 3-17.

[51] Baxter, L., Thorne, E. and Mitchell, E. (2001) *Small voices big noises: Lay involvement in health research – Lessons from other fields*, Exeter: Washington Singer Press, available at http://www.conres.co.uk/pdf/small_voices.pdf

[52] Morris, J. (1994) *The shape of things to come? User led social services*, Social Services Forum Paper 3, London: National Institute for Social Work.

[53] Fisher, M. (2002) 'The role of service users in problem formulation and technical aspects of research', *Social Work Education*, vol 21, no 3, pp 305-12.

[54] Evans, C. and Carmichael, A. (2002) *Users' Best Value: A guide to user involvement good practice in Best Value reviews*, York: York Publishing Services.

[55] Wilson, A. and Beresford, P. (2000) '"Anti-oppressive practice": emancipation or appropriation', *British Journal of Social Work*, vol 30, no 5, pp 553-73.

Index

Other Knowledge Reviews available from SCIE

KNOWLEDGE REVIEW 1
Learning and teaching in social work education: Assessment
Beth R. Crisp, Mark R. Anderson, Joan Orme and Pam Green Lister
1 904812 00 7
November 2003

KNOWLEDGE REVIEW 2
The adoption of looked after children: A scoping review of research
Alan Rushton
1 904812 01 5
November 2003

KNOWLEDGE REVIEW 4
Innovative, tried and tested: A review of good practice in fostering
Clive Sellick and Darren Howell
1 904812 03 1
November 2003

KNOWLEDGE REVIEW 5
Fostering success: An exploration of the research literature in foster care
Kate Wilson, Ian Sinclair, Claire Taylor, Andrew Pithouse and Clive Sellick
1 904812 04 X
November 2003